DARLENE
WILKINSON

SECRETS

of the

VINE

for Women

Breaking Through to Abundance

MULTNOMAH
BOOKS

Our God is so awesome! Enjoy,
Darlene Marie Wilkinson
2011

SECRETS OF THE VINE FOR WOMEN
PUBLISHED BY MULTNOMAH BOOKS
12265 Oracle Boulevard, Suite 200
Colorado Springs, Colorado 80921

All Scripture quotations, unless otherwise indicated, are taken from the Holy Bible, New King James Version © 1982 by Thomas Nelson Inc. Used by permission. All rights reserved. Scripture quotations marked (NIV) are taken from the Holy Bible, New International Version®. NIV®. Copyright 1973, 1978, 1984 by International Bible Society. Used by permission of Zondervan Publishing House. All rights reserved.

Secrets of the Vine® is a registered trademark of Random House Inc.

ISBN 978-160142-397-9

Cover design by Kristopher K. Orr

Published by WaterBrook Multnomah, an imprint of the Crown Publishing Group, a division of Random House Inc., New York.

MULTNOMAH and its mountain colophon are trademarks of Random House Inc.

Printed in the United States of America
2011—First Trade Paperback Edition

10 9 8 7 6 5 4 3 2 1

SPECIAL SALES
Most WaterBrook Multnomah books are available at special quantity discounts when purchased in bulk by corporations, organizations, and special-interest groups. Custom imprinting or excerpting can also be done to fit special needs. For information, please e-mail SpecialMarkets@WaterBrookMultnomah.com or call 1-800-603-7051.

Table of Contents

Preface: *A Place to Grow* 5

Chapter One: *A Spiritual Harvest* 7

Chapter Two: *The Touch of Abundance* 19

Chapter Three: *Lifted by Love* 33

Chapter Four: *Making Room for More* 53

Chapter Five: *The Miracle of Much Fruit* 73

Chapter Six: *Your Father's Prize* 97

Appendix: *Three Seasons in God's Vineyard* . . .111

Study Guide 113

A Place to Grow

Dear Reader,

Thank you for picking up *Secrets of the Vine for Women.* I'm praying that you, along with thousands of others, will remember this little book as a turning point in your life.

A turning point, a pivotal experience, something that leaves you forever changed—that's what so many women are looking for today. And I can tell you from personal experience that Jesus' words in John 15 are life changing! In this conversation in a vineyard the night before He died, Jesus showed His followers how God would be at work to bring each of them to a truly abundant life.

I invite you to step with me into that vineyard and listen carefully to what Jesus said. And as you read, may you be in awe of your Father's faithfulness and greatness, because incredible spiritual abundance is His plan today for you, too.

With affection,

Darlene Marie

*"I have come that they
may have life, and that they may
have it more abundantly."*

John 10:10

CHAPTER ONE

A Spiritual Harvest

The train creaked to a stop. A young woman standing ready at the door gazed out over the rooftop of the railway station to the golden hills of Tuscany. "How beautiful it is!" she sighed. The bustling cities of the north were behind her now. Finally, she was home.

Descending to the wooden platform, she felt her weariness slip away. Eagerly, she scanned the sea of faces until she saw him. Her father, a tall, bronzed man, was easy to find in a crowd, and she had sought him out many times. When she caught his eye, he rushed toward her, arms outstretched, and wrapped her in an embrace.

"Welcome, my beautiful girl!" he cried. "I've missed you so much!"

It didn't take long to have her bags sent on ahead. As usual, her father wanted to take her on foot out of the village and up the twisting lanes that led to their home. Leaving the station, they walked hand in hand, talking and laughing. He asked about her life in the city. She asked about the approaching harvest. And as they talked and walked, she reveled in the warm sun of an Italian autumn.

At the crest of the hill her eyes fell upon a familiar scene— her father's vineyard, rolling away in neatly tended rows. She had grown up following her father as he worked up and down those rows. And since childhood she'd known that her father was well-respected throughout the region as a champion vinedresser. But at her first view of the vineyard, now heavy with fruit, her breath caught in her throat.

"Papa!" she exclaimed. "I've never seen such a promising crop!" She walked down a row to look more closely. Huge clusters of dark, satiny grapes hung from every branch.

Turning back to her father, she saw the pleasure on his face. "You must be very proud," she said. "I still remember the wretched state of these plants when we first came here. How diligently you have worked all these years to produce such an incredible yield!"

She tucked her arm in his, steering them toward the house. "I'm so glad to be home to celebrate this harvest with you!" she said. This was the most anticipated season in the vineyard, and she didn't want to miss any of it. She could hardly wait.

The young woman in our story has, for many years, observed the tending of her father's vineyard. She is well acquainted with all that is required to produce a harvest. And she knows how much a great harvest of prize-winning grapes will mean to her father.

You, on the other hand, may never have walked through a vineyard or even seen grapes hanging from a branch. For that reason, in the chapters to come we'll revisit our young friend and her father as the grape harvest approaches. I want you to feel the sun, smell the earth, and touch the rough leaves of the grape plant. I want you to celebrate with them as they anticipate a bumper crop.

Why should you think about grapes?

Because the truths I want to explore with you in this little book, based on Jesus' teachings in John 15, have a lot to do with grapes and how they grow. The vineyard we're interested in is a spiritual picture rather than an actual place. But I promise that the lessons you learn there will be so real to you that they will change your life forever.

Abundance— a life as full as possible of God's best.

I can make such a promise because our teacher is Jesus,

and His words are part of His last conversation with His friends on the night before He died. What He said surprised His disciples. I'm sure it wasn't what they wanted to hear. But Jesus knew it was what they desperately needed to hear. Otherwise they would never experience the abundant life God had in mind for them.

Abundance—a life as full as possible of God's best. It's the picture God has in mind for us, too. Unfortunately, if we don't understand what God does to bring that wonderful harvest about, we can actually work against His good hand in our lives without ever knowing it.

But then Jesus makes a string of disturbing announcements.

By the time you finish this little book, some important principles of how abundance happens in your life will become clear, and you'll learn how to cooperate with your Father's hand—for your greatest fulfillment, and for His glory.

For example, you'll discover how He intervenes when sin is holding you back. You'll understand how He responds when your own good intentions are leading you astray. You'll learn, perhaps for the first time, just how much He longs to enjoy intimate fellowship with you, and you'll have a clear idea of what you need to do to make that relationship happen. And finally, you'll know for certain that you can expect more lasting results from your life than you ever thought possible.

Listen in now as Jesus talks quietly with His friends over dinner.

DINNER REVELATIONS

It is the night of the Passover. Jesus and His inner circle of followers are eating together in the upper room. They have much to celebrate. The events leading up to this meal have confirmed to the disciples that Jesus is the long-awaited Messiah. They're convinced that by tomorrow, if not before, Jesus will give the word and usher in His new kingdom. And it's a kingdom they can't wait to be part of.

He was thinking of His love for them. And I believe He was thinking of you.

The atmosphere is electric. But then Jesus makes a string of disturbing announcements: One of the disciples will betray Him. One will deny Him. He is leaving, and they can't follow. And the final, shattering disclosure: that "the ruler of this world is coming"—and it will not be Him.

The men are speechless. Just moments ago they were poised for a great future. Now Jesus seems to be saying that it will never happen. All their dreams and plans have turned into a crushing disappointment.

At the end of the evening, Jesus says, "Arise, let us go from here." As He leads them out into the night, questions and doubts swirl in their minds. By the light of lamps and torches, they follow Him quietly through the winding streets of Jerusalem, down to a lower gate of the city, and out into the Kidron Valley.

We anticipate a bright tomorrow, only to find ourselves peering into a dark today.

Here, they walk through ancient vineyards, carefully tended for generations and famously productive. Jesus and His followers find their way through the rows of vines on their way to their destination—the Garden of Gethsemane on a nearby hill.

It is in this very vineyard, many scholars believe, that Jesus paused to deliver His parting message to His disciples. And here, as He so often did, Jesus used an earthy, familiar illustration to impart timeless spiritual truths. Before, He had talked about water, lambs, coins, runaway sons, and bread. This time Jesus talked about fruit. "I am the vine, you are the branches," He said (John 15:5).

As He talked, I believe He was pointing to a branch, to

leaves, to a vine. But He was looking right at His friends. With every word, He was thinking of His love for them, of the challenges they'd face, of the amazing and specific future God had in mind for each one of them.

And I believe He was thinking of you.

A Picture of His Plan

One of my favorite childhood memories is of our family working around a table over a 500-piece puzzle during the Christmas holidays. I loved sorting through my pile of pieces—blue ones, green ones, multicolored ones—trying to find a perfect fit. Piece by irregular piece, the picture slowly came to life. Of course, every once in a while I'd turn the box lid over and take a long hard look at the painting on the cover. There it was—the gorgeous finished picture we were all working toward.

> *Every touch of His hand is intended to bring us to a place of great spiritual abundance.*

That box lid was proof that no matter how stuck we were at the moment, our individual pieces were made to fit together. Eventually, we knew, we'd have spread out in front of us a grand scene—a harbor full of colorful sailing boats, maybe, or a Swiss mountain village. We didn't have to guess at our goal. We could see where we were supposed to end up. And we could see that it would be beautiful.

You've probably been around that table with your family many times, too. And like me, you probably can't imagine how difficult those puzzles would have been to complete without having the big picture right there at hand.

That night in the vineyard, Jesus "turned the box lid over" and showed us the big picture. He wanted us to see—no matter what circumstance we're in at the moment—what God the Father is trying to accomplish in and through us for eternity. He wanted us to know how to respond to His will. He wanted us to remember that every touch of His hand is intended to bring us to a place of great spiritual abundance.

Women consistently express a desire to go deeper.

And to accomplish all that, Jesus showed us a picture of a vineyard.

Using the illustrations of a vinedresser, a vine, a branch, and fruit, Jesus told us plainly that He wants something specific from us. And He wants it so much that He continually intervenes in our lives—sometimes even with pain—to make it happen.

Maybe you can identify with what those disappointed disciples experienced that night. So many women can. We know what it's like to anticipate a bright tomorrow, only to find ourselves peering into a dark today. Things are going along according to plan, then for no apparent reason we find ourselves ambushed by confusion or pain. We wonder, *Why is this happening? Has God forgotten me? What on earth is He up to in my life?*

If you have already read *Secrets of the Vine,* you know the answer. If not, what I want to share with you may come as a surprise—yet it's a surprise full of promise. Either way, if what you want most is greater fruitfulness and service and impact for God in your life, then the teachings of the vineyard are for you.

WHERE WOMEN WALK

You might be wondering why I decided to write *Secrets of the Vine for Women.* After all, *Secrets of the Vine* is already a publishing success. And it turns out that it has been even more widely read by women than men. Bruce was flooded with letters from women saying things like, "This book felt like a big hug from God," and "*Secrets* explained what I experienced just last week!" Everywhere I go I meet women who have been changed by the truths of John 15.

But in fact, the special appeal of this message for women is the very reason I feel compelled to pick up my pen (and yes, I start out by writing in longhand!). Wherever I teach on this subject, woman consistently express a desire to go deeper. They want to learn more about how Jesus' vineyard conversation applies to their experiences as women in today's world. In short, they want to continue the conversation!

I realized how much I actually resisted what God was doing to help me flourish.

And so do I.

In the pages to come I will introduce you to some women like yourself. They are mothers, daughters, wives, sisters, and singles with one thing in common: They believe God does have a loving and amazing plan for greater fruitfulness in their lives…and they want it with all their heart!

The message of *Secrets of the Vine for Women* is also a very personal one for me. More than any other teaching I've explored, it has dramatically changed the way I respond to challenging circumstances in my life. I realized how much I actually resisted what God was doing to help me flourish. It wasn't until I understood what Jesus taught about God's ways with us that I went from questioning God's motives to embracing His plan for my life. The best word I can come up with for the result is *abundance*.

If that's what you want with all your heart, please join me in the pages ahead.

"I am the true vine, and
My Father is the vinedresser."

JOHN 15:1

CHAPTER TWO

The Touch of Abundance

While they waited for supper to be served, the young woman and her father stepped out onto the tiled courtyard. The vineyard was still visible in the dusky light. In just a few days, workers from miles around would arrive to assist with the harvest.

She watched and listened as her father pointed out various changes in the landscape before them.

"Do you remember the view from here when I bought this estate?" her father asked.

She contemplated his question. "I remember more rows of vines than I'd ever seen. And I remember leaves. I remember a lot of scraggly—"

"But do you remember grapes?" her father asked.

"Only a few, Papa. A grape here or there." She was smiling. He was smiling, too. They'd had this conversation before.

Now, gazing out across the grape-laden vines, she remembers a morning long ago . . .

She's a little girl, playing with clumps of earth as she watches her father work patiently on a branch.

Peering up at her father from under a straw hat, she exclaims, "But I don't see any grapes here, Papa. You said we were going to grow grapes!"

Her father laughs. "You have good eyes, don't you?" He straightens up to look around. "These branches don't have any fruit. Not yet. They need lots of patient care and tending. But one day, my daughter, one day. You wait and see . . ."

One thing that any gardener knows is that a bumper crop doesn't just happen. It takes a plan. It takes time, work, and plenty of close attention. The vinedresser in our story knows that. He is personally involved with each branch in his vineyard because he wants to see each branch flourish and grow.

Now listen carefully to the words of Jesus that night in the vineyard. These verses may be familiar to you. But receive them this time as a first-person description of your Father at work in His garden.

> *"I am the true vine, and My Father is the vinedresser. Every branch in Me that does*

*not bear fruit He takes away; and every
branch that bears fruit He prunes, that it
may bear more fruit. I am the vine, you are
the branches. He who abides in Me, and I in
him, bears much fruit. By this My Father is
glorified, that you bear much fruit."*

JOHN 15:1–2, 5, 8

Notice that your Father has a plan—the biggest, most beautiful harvest possible.

Notice telltale signs of His utter dedication—not one branch is overlooked.

Feel the singular passion that He pours into His special object of affection—the branches.

From Him will come the power and provision to accomplish His Father's work.

In this chapter we'll look more closely at the picture of the vineyard Jesus described. Because every word He said is really about you—your life today, your relationship with God, and your amazing future.

YOUR LIFE AS A BRANCH

Three distinct persons are represented in the picture that Jesus gave that night in the vineyard.

1. *Jesus is the vine* (v. 1). In a vineyard, the vine is the main stem or trunk that grows up out of the ground. Interestingly, the vine doesn't produce the fruit—the branches do that.

    Jesus is telling His disciples that He is their source of life. From Him will come the power and provision to accomplish His Father's work on earth.

2. *God the Father is the Vinedresser* (v. 1). A vinedresser is the owner or tender of the vineyard. He cares for each branch in such a way that it produces the most grapes possible.

    Since the role of a grower is so much like that of a parent, it shouldn't surprise us that Jesus identified God the Father as the Vinedresser.

3. *Every follower of Christ is a branch* (v. 5). In a vineyard, several branches grow from each vine. They are tied to stakes or wires for support and care. Every new shoot, leaf, or tendril is carefully tended with the

harvest to come in mind. And what the vinedresser has in mind is fruit.

Are you a follower of Christ? Then you're a branch. For your whole life, God has been purposefully at work on your branch like a passionate, attentive vinedresser. Every intervention in your life circumstances has been with a goal in mind. And what a goal it is—a great harvest for God's glory!

For too many years, bearing fruit as a Christian was a vague concept to me.

You can tell Jesus didn't want His disciples to miss the point because He summarized the meaning of His vineyard picture again in verse 16:

> *"You did not choose Me, but I chose you and appointed you that you should go and bear fruit, and that your fruit should remain."*

Jesus was leaving them—and us!—with a very important assignment. He wants us to bear spiritual fruit that will last forever.

But what exactly is fruit?

A PASSION FOR MORE

After she read *Secrets of the Vine,* a woman named Sarena sent Bruce a note. "I don't have another day to waste," she said. "I've wasted too many years already. I want to be a passionate Christian. I want my life to be an overflowing basket for God."

I understand Sarena's urgency about doing something significant with her life. But I have to admit that for too many years, bearing fruit as a Christian was a vague concept to me. I thought it was something pastors and evangelists did mostly from the platform in front of large crowds. And I was absolutely terrified of speaking in public!

If I could hand you a piece of paper and ask you to list one "fruit" that was part of your life yesterday, what would you write down?

If you are giving this page a blank stare, perhaps it's because you are uncertain, as I was for so long, as to how to understand fruit in a woman's life. You may be as eager as Sarena to bear fruit for God, yet you may have no idea what that activity actually looks like.

Let's look at the New Testament for help. In the following three verses, one word occurs repeatedly in association with the idea of spiritual fruitfulness.

Ephesians 5:11—"Have no fellowship with the *unfruitful works* of darkness."

Colossians 1:10—"Walk worthy of the Lord, fully pleasing Him, being *fruitful* in *every good work.*"

Titus 3:14—"And let our people also learn to maintain *good works,* to meet urgent needs, that they may not be *unfruitful.*"

I'm sure it's plain to you now. A fruit for God is a good work for Him—something you do that helps someone else and brings God glory.

Now if I ask you to list a good work you've done recently, your pen should flow more easily. Or maybe you're like me and what comes to mind first is a work for God with someone else's name and face on it . . .

CREATED FOR THIS

I think of Jan, for instance. Her seventy-year old mother-in-law fell last week and broke her leg in two places. Even with three active teenagers, Jan is patiently and joyfully doing everything she can to nurse her mother-in-law back to health.

I think, too, of Jennifer, a full-time office worker. Somebody once described her work environment as the "Snake Pit." Yet everyone notices her positive attitude and patience with others (including a demanding boss). And they know their clients count on Jennifer because of her integrity under pressure.

And Regina, mother of four small boys. Her husband is on the road a lot, but she works hard to make coming home the best part of his week, including having the children ready and waiting at the door with hugs for Daddy.

And Teri, a breath of encouragement. She is confined to a wheelchair because of a car accident. She spends a lot of time each week praying for the needs in her local congregation. When friends visit, they usually leave saying the same thing: "I went to encourage Teri and left encouraged myself."

What a great question to ask yourself: Have I done what I could?

Too many women I know think of singing in the choir or teaching a Sunday school class as the *real* good works, and the ordinary tasks of serving others throughout the day as somehow less significant. Even the disciples had that problem.

Imagine how Mary must have felt when they criticized her for anointing Jesus' head with her vial of perfume (Mark 14:3–9). The Bible says they were indignant and "criticized her sharply" (v. 5). Ouch!

You see, the disciples thought the oil would have had a more spiritual use if it had been sold and the money given to charity. But Jesus stepped in to the argument. "Let her alone," He said. "She has done a good work for Me" (v. 6).

So we need to change our mind about the good works ready and waiting for each of us to offer up to God. Our opportunities don't very often require a platform, or an extraordinary talent, or an unusual opportunity. They require a heart that is ready to do a good work for Jesus at a moment's notice.

Perhaps the reason the Bible doesn't record all possible good works is that there are too many to list! Yet what the Bible does say about good works is even more amazing. I'm thinking about Paul's statement in Ephesians 2:

> *For we are His workmanship, created in Christ Jesus for good works, which God prepared beforehand that we should walk in them.*
>
> v. 10

What an incredible thought! You and I have been created for the purpose of doing good works. God designed you, He gifted you, and He placed you in the world so that the fruit of your life would have an everlasting impact. He even prepared those activities for you before you were born.

Out of all the centuries in time, this is the generation into which God chose to place you. Of course, you had nothing to do with the country in which you were born or the family you were born into. But clearly God placed you in His world at this particular time so that you could do something special.

Now I want you to notice what Jesus went on to say about Mary's simple act of selflessness: "She has done what she could" (Mark 14:8). What a great question to ask yourself at the end of a day! *Have I done what I could?*

I encourage you to ask God to show you every day what your specially prepared works are, and to help you do them for His glory. Once a woman sees the eternity-plan of the Vinedresser surfacing in every ordinary day, it's hard to go back to that boring old life you used to walk through.

Let me give you a personal example.

WALKING IN GOOD WORKS

I remember thinking about Ephesians 2:10 one day when suddenly the words *that we should walk in them* leaped out at me. Walk in good works? What was I to make of that?

At the time, we lived in a small blue house where I spent my days caring for the needs of two small children and a busy husband. Bruce was beginning to travel more and more as the Lord blessed his teaching ministry, Walk Thru the Bible. For me, on the other hand, "travel" usually meant a dash to the grocery store or doctor's office, and then it was back to the little blue house. My purse, my wardrobe, and most of my dreams smelled of graham crackers.

Can you relate?

One morning I heard a knock at the door. A young mom from down the street was standing there in tears. When I invited her in, she told me that her three misbehaving children had pushed her to the end of her rope. She needed help, but didn't know where to turn.

I can still picture us sitting together drinking hot tea at the kitchen table. Since I had recently been reading in Proverbs during my quiet time, it felt natural to show her several verses that gave wisdom about family discipline. She left an hour or so later, encouraged and committed to dealing with her children by using God's principles.

That was the day I understood what the Bible meant by walking in good works. I was busy doing the works at home that God had called me to do for that season of my life. To my Lord, they were beautiful, and honoring, and enough. When the time was right, God didn't suddenly drop me into an auditorium or an international travel schedule. He brought me another mother in tears about her children. She was standing right in front of me, on the porch of my little blue house.

Picture yourself getting up in the morning and walking through your day. (You may feel like sprinting or running through your day is a little more realistic!) Look over your list of tasks and routines and people who depend on you. Every activity represents a good work for you to walk in— a work that is yours to do, and yours to give the Lord. You just have to be ready to see it, and ready to do it with your whole heart.

I think it's interesting that Jesus said to "go and *bear* fruit," not to "go and *find* fruit." When you think about it, bringing life into the world is something women have understood since Eve ("be fruitful and multiply"). And it is our privilege and honor, no matter where we are, to bear spiritual fruit for Him. And a lot of it!

Jesus said, "By this my Father is glorified, that you bear *much fruit*" (John 15:8).

BASKETS OF ABUNDANCE

Think about it: It's not our good intentions to be fruitful that bring our Father glory. It's not even how hard we try. It is how much fruit comes from our branch. Each branch bears a different amount of fruit, and all fruit honors God. But God's greatest glory comes from the ones who bear much fruit.

If you look closely at Jesus' teaching in John 15, you'll notice four levels of fruit bearing:

Level 1—no fruit ("every branch in Me that *does not bear fruit,*" v. 2, emphasis added).

Level 2—fruit ("every branch that bears *fruit,*" v. 2).

Level 3—more fruit ("that it may bear *more fruit,*" v. 2).

Level 4—much fruit ("bears *much fruit,*" vv. 5, 8).

Where do you think your level of fruit bearing is at this very moment? If the Master Vinedresser harvested your branch this year for His glory, how much honor would He receive? A lot? Some? A little? None?

If you sense that you are among those branches that could bear a lot more fruit, be encouraged! God cares so much about the outcome of your fruitfulness that you can count on Him to work continuously in your life toward a huge harvest for Him.

In the chapters to come, we're going to learn what God does to take us from one level of fruitfulness to the next, and then to the next. We'll call His methods "secrets," but really they are very simple truths that every believer can understand. Once you know them, I think you'll agree that a life of overflowing spiritual abundance is God's dream for every one of His children.

*For whom the L*ORD *loves*
He corrects, just as a father the son
in whom he delights.

PROVERBS 3:12

CHAPTER THREE

Lifted by Love

During the night, the sound of distant thunder awoke the young woman. She lay in bed, listening to a scattering of raindrops on the leaves outside her window. It was not good news. Only two days remained before the harvest, and the weather was not cooperating.

Outside, lightning flashed. The young woman knew her father was awake and concerned, too.

She still remembered the first time a severe storm hit the vineyard. She'd followed her father on his rounds as he carried a bucket of water. "Look at this branch," he said, pointing to one that was half buried in mud. She watched as he knelt down and set to work. He gently washed the branch off and tied it up to the trellis again.

"What are you doing?" she asked.

"Helping this branch get better," he said.

"Is it sick?"

"Yes, you could say that."

"Does it have a temperature, Papa?"

"No. It fell into the dirt in a storm."

"Doesn't it want to grow any more grapes?"

"Of course it does! In fact, someday it will grow more grapes than you could eat in a week!"

Now as the young woman listened to the plinking of the rain, she thought about how gentle and caring her father had been to each branch as he went about his work.

And with that thought, she drifted back to sleep.

———

I t didn't seem like such a terrible thing. At least, not while I was in the department store on my lunch break. The cashier had misread the price tag and undercharged me several dollars. I recall thinking, "What a blessing! I got a real discount!" At the time, Bruce was a seminary student and I was working full-time to help pay the bills. *The Lord must be providing a little extra through her mistake,* I decided.

But as I walked out the door, an uninvited question burst into my thoughts: *What's the biblical term for what you just did?*

The answer flashed through my mind: *stealing.*

I wish I could tell you that I turned around and made things right, but I didn't. Actually, I decided that the store had lots of money, and Bruce and I didn't, and I put it out of my mind.

But when I crawled into bed that night, my unexpected "blessing" kept coming to mind, and I tossed and turned for hours. In the morning, I dashed off to work promising myself to return the money on my lunch hour.

At noon, halfway through my sandwich, I reached for my pocket New Testament. Opening it at random, I read James 4:17: "Therefore, to him who knows to do good and does not do it, to him it is sin." (So much for random reading!)

But I still didn't go back to that store.

Instead, I returned to work only to go home early because of a terrible headache. By now, I felt both physically and spiritually ill. And angry, too. *This is ridiculous,* I fumed. *It's only a few dollars! Why should I torture and humiliate myself over so little?*

> *Those few stolen dollars were a symptom of a very unattractive pattern in my life.*

But as I lay on my bed, I saw that it was not a little thing. In fact, those few stolen dollars were really just the latest symptom of a growing and very unattractive pattern in my life. I saw attitudes of rebellion, resistance, and compromise that I had been excusing for too long. No wonder I'd been feeling so spiritually unmotivated.

Has God ever seemed to ambush you with the truth like that?

This chapter is about how our Father intervenes to rescue us from the mud of our own wrong choices. Jesus' teachings in the vineyard show us that unaddressed sin in our lives is like dirt on the grape branch of our lives. It cuts out the air and sun, and makes fruit bearing nearly impossible. We need help!

The good news is that our Father the Vinedresser has a plan for our future. And the plan is as wonderful as it is surprising.

LIFTED BY LOVE

In His vineyard teaching, Jesus spoke very directly about what God does with the branch that is barren:

> *"Every branch in Me that does not bear fruit*
> *He takes away."*
>
> V. 2

Since Jesus identified every branch "in Me," we know He was speaking only about believers. The New Testament often describes the believer as a person who is "in Christ" (for examples, see Ephesians 2:10 and Philippians 3:9).

But "takes away"? That doesn't sound very promising, does it?

Some have taught that God literally discards an unfruitful Christian. But a closer look at the meaning of the Greek word *airo*—here translated as "takes away" or "cuts off"—shows a much different and more hopeful picture.

If you've read *Secrets of the Vine,* you remember how Bruce's study of the original language, along with a chance conversation with a grape grower, turned on the lights for him on this passage. A stronger rendering of *airo* is "lift up" or "take up." (Other New Testament passages support this reading of *airo*. The same word is used, for example, when the disciples took up twelve baskets of food after the feeding of the five thousand in Matthew 14:20, and when Simon was forced to carry Christ's cross in Matthew 27:32.)

God loves us too much not to intervene when we slide off course.

And according to the California vineyard keeper, "lift up" is exactly what growers do to grape branches that are trailing in the dirt. The branch is too valuable to cut off and throw away. Instead, the vinedresser carefully lifts the dirty branches, washes them off, and ties them up in the sun so they can begin producing again.

You and I are too valuable to be discarded by our Father, too. Instead of throwing us away, He will step in to bring us back to fruitfulness. But what does this process look like in our lives?

That's the wonderful news of the first secret of the vine.

First Secret of the Vine:

If your life consistently bears no fruit,
God will intervene to discipline you
so you will bear fruit.

The truth is that God loves us too much not to intervene when we slide off course. He pursues us and disciplines us through our whole lives because He still has a plan for our best. And that best, says Jesus, looks a lot like a branch full of beautiful grapes.

Training Days

Wouldn't it be great if we could just experience God's best in life without a little redirection? Then again, wouldn't it be great if our kids would do the right thing without ever needing a reminder from us? Or maybe several reminders? Or maybe losing a coveted privilege? Ouch!

You see how easy it is to go from the need to bring correction to the subject of...pain?!

Scripture uses words parents are familiar with, like *discipline* and *chastening,* to describe how God redirects His children. For example, these verses in Hebrews:

> If you endure chastening, God deals with you as with sons; for what son is there whom a father does not chasten? But if you are without chastening, of which all have become partakers, then you are illegitimate and not sons.

HEBREWS 12:7–8

We'd like to think that God the Father would choose a disciplinary response that got wonderful results without pain. But not so. Hebrews assures us of that:

> *Now no chastening seems to be joyful for the present, but painful; nevertheless, afterward it yields the peaceable fruit of righteousness to those who have been trained by it.*

V. 11

If you're like me, you have a strong dislike for pain. I am

on "red alert" the moment I feel it. But the truth is, years ago I used the same "red alert" response to teach my young children. First a warning: "Jessica, honey! Don't touch the stove! It's hot!" If that didn't work, a smack on her little hand came next: "Jessica, listen and obey! I said don't touch the stove! You'll burn yourself!"

You understand what I'm saying, don't you? The pain of that smack on your child's hand has only one purpose— you sincerely want to prevent her from experiencing a much greater pain. The goal of your discipline is that your child will "be trained by it."

We should never think that all suffering comes from God.

Of course, God doesn't physically smack our straying hands. Instead, He works through people and circumstances to train up His children. If we respond positively to the pain, we turn more and more in His direction. And the result is the "peaceable fruit of righteousness."

We should never think that all suffering comes from God. God is the source of every good and perfect gift (James 1:17). But we happen to live in a fallen world where disease, evil people, and natural disasters can strike at any time. God understands our pain so deeply that He chose to send His

40

own Son to bring us redemption and eternal life. Yet the Bible makes it clear that God will use discomfort or suffering in our lives to get our attention, to turn us away from harm, and to turn us toward abundance.

Does our Father *want* to cause us discomfort or anguish? Of course not.

Will our Father stop pursuing us with His best? Not even when we break His heart.

And not even if we don't pay attention the first time.

"Whom the Lord Loves"

As every mom knows, there's a big difference in how you discipline Johnny if he spends his Sunday school offering on candy once, and how you discipline him if he is stealing grievously and repeatedly. In the same way, God's discipline is always in proportion to the seriousness of the sin. Jesus taught the principle of escalating discipline in Matthew 18:15–17, and we see it repeated in Hebrews.

Notice the underlined words in the following verses. They show three different labels for discipline, suggesting increasing degrees of intensity:

And you have forgotten the exhortation which speaks to you as to sons:

"My son, do not despise the chastening of the LORD,
nor be discouraged when you are <u>rebuked</u> by Him;
For whom the LORD loves He <u>chastens</u>, and <u>scourges</u>
every son whom He receives."

HEBREWS 12:5-6

A rebuke is a spoken warning. If you think about it, you'll agree that in an average day, 99 percent of a young mother's discipline comes through words of rebuke. We may receive rebukes from a friend, a pastor, a word of Scripture, or directly from the Holy Spirit.

Discipline is a family word that proves our Father's love and assures us that we are His children.

Chastening seems to show a more serious level of discipline (verse 11 in the same chapter describes it as "painful"). I've experienced this level of discipline as emotional anxiety, distress, or an ongoing circumstance of extreme frustration.

The third level, scourging, points to physical pain. Scourging is what the Roman soldiers did to Jesus with whips. Spiritually, this level of discipline is probably reserved for Christians who are living in open sin, having lost any concern for what God wants or how their actions are affecting others.

You and I can trust that God's ways with us are always wise and good, and with one goal in mind. The psalmist wrote, "Before I was afflicted I went astray, but now I keep Your word" (Psalm 119:67). God's goal is always our obedience to His will, because in His will is our best.

Sadly, Christians you and I know are suffering every day unnecessarily because they have not heard or acted on the truth of God's discipline. They misinterpret unwanted circumstances and emotions as random events when they are actually God's efforts to set them free from sin and bring them back to fruitfulness.

> *God's discipline is always in proportion to the seriousness of the sin.*

Some of us even act on the lie that we can hang onto ongoing sin, bear fruit for God . . . and experience no other unwanted consequences. As a result, we experience unnecessary suffering and a broken relationship with our heavenly Father.

But it doesn't have to be that way. Just ask some women who have been there . . .

Don't Mix These Words Up

Be sure not to confuse God's discipline with punishment. Discipline is for God's children; punishment is for His enemies. Punishment includes anger, wrath, and the intent to make someone pay for their offenses. When Christ hung on the cross over two thousand years ago, He took on Himself the punishment we deserved for our sins. He "bore our sins in His own body on the tree, that we, having died to sins, might live for righteousness" (1 Peter 2:24). The moment we believe by faith that through His death and resurrection Jesus paid the full penalty for our sins, the word punishment ceases to apply to us.

However, even though our sins are forgiven, their consequences will bring harm to us, to others, and to our relationship with God. That's why His loving correction is so important. *Discipline* is a family word that proves our Father's love and assures us that we are His children.

In Him we have redemption through His blood, the forgiveness of sins, according to the riches of His grace.

EPHESIANS 1:7

STORIES ON THE ROAD TO BOUNTIFUL

"I'd been feeling unexplainable frustration and anger even though things were going well," wrote Nicole, after reading *Secrets of the Vine*. "I couldn't figure out what was causing the feelings until one night when I sat down to write in my journal. After a two-page prayer, I saw it clearly. I had been unable to forgive myself and others for some things that had happened, and so I assumed that God wasn't able to forgive me either."

As Nicole poured out her tears and her confession to God, He began to bring back the relief that had been missing. She says she feels a new sense of peace now. "Just doing the dishes feels more restful. It is so good to be personal with God again."

She took brave steps toward a God-honoring life. But she continued to have a sexual relationship with her boyfriend.

Then there's Amy, a single mom who came to the Lord about a year ago when a Christian drama group visited her Atlanta neighborhood. She left behind a life of drug and alcohol addiction. She went back to school to earn her GED. She took many brave steps toward a God-honoring life. But she continued to have a sexual relationship with her boyfriend.

God didn't deal with Amy on this issue the moment she became saved. Instead, He allowed her time to grow and to understand His ways and His will for her life. "Then came a gentle rebuke in the form of a friend's concern," she says. "And when I went for counseling, the pastor was even more frank with me about what God requires of His children in the way of sexual purity."

You may be one choice away, as I was, from a fresh start with God.

But still, Amy didn't want to change this part of her life. "I was afraid of losing my boyfriend and he didn't want to marry me." The pressure on Amy's life increased when she wanted to work with the junior high group at church. She knew she couldn't do so until she resolved this issue.

"Then things got even tougher for me," she admits. "My boyfriend betrayed me with another woman. I lost my job at the library. I felt like my whole life was falling apart. And that did it. I repented—and probably just in time." Since then, Amy has been finding many ministry opportunities helping other young women who are struggling with the same issues.

At a recent conference I attended, a woman gave this incredible testimony. In her case, she had allowed God's discipline to progress to a much more intense level:

"Six months ago I was diagnosed with an incurable disease and told to get my affairs in order. I went to my pastor, who wisely asked, 'Are there any regrets in your life?' After some reflection, I told him I'd held a deep grudge against my sister for more than ten years, even though my bitterness had harmed myself and others. 'Are you willing to forgive her now?' asked the pastor. When I said yes, he led me through a time of confession and repentance for my anger, hurtfulness and bitterness. Then I went to my sister and asked if we could talk about our broken relationship. I confessed my grudge, and told her I knew that my bitterness toward her was sin. Then I begged for her forgiveness. She did forgive me, and we shared a very meaningful time together. I left feeling cleansed and free to love her again. Within weeks, my symptoms unexpectedly disappeared. In fact, the doctors can find no trace of the disease. That's why I now firmly believe that ongoing sin in a Christian's life has both spiritual and physical consequences."

That experience showed me the source of my spiritual barrenness, and it revealed to me God's ongoing desire for my restoration.

Your story may not be as dramatic as these. Or it may be

much more dramatic! God has such an amazing adventure ahead for each of us. Whatever your circumstances right now, I imagine that if you looked back over your own life, you could identify a time when serious, unaddressed sin cut you off from God's blessings and put you directly in the path of His discipline.

I walked up to a very surprised store manager and handed him his dollars along with my apology.

Don't let God's precious investment in you go to waste! Ask, *What did I learn in those times? What do I now know about God that I didn't before? How have I changed for the better?*

You might decide you are experiencing your Father's discipline right now. If so, I encourage you to carefully evaluate your beliefs and actions. You may be one choice away, as I was, from a fresh start with God.

The Waters of Repentance

Looking back on my department store misadventure, I'm almost glad I didn't immediately return those few dollars. Why? Because that experience showed me the source of my spiritual barrenness, and it revealed to me God's ongoing desire for my restoration.

Old Obstacles, New Breakthrough Beliefs

adapted from *Secrets of the Vine Bible Study*

We never have to be enslaved by sin, repeating the same destructive patterns (Romans 6:11–12). But at times, our human thinking can hold us hostage to lies. Choose the false beliefs that most seem to be keeping you from making a change today. Let the Bible help you discover a new breakthrough truth, and write it down (in your own words) in your journal.

1. The "I Can Outlast God" Strategy. *You believe that God will eventually give up and leave you alone.* Psalm 139:7–12; Luke 15:1–7.

2. The "If You Can't Beat 'Em, Join 'Em" Defense. *You believe that you can't give up your sin. You've tried many times; why try again?* Romans 6:14; 1 Corinthians 10:1–13; 2 Peter 2:9.

3. The "Big, Mean God" Assumption. *You believe that God is wrong to cause you pain no matter what you've done.* Job 5:17–18; Psalm 145:8–9; Ezekiel 33:11; Hebrews 12:5–17.

4. The "Ostrich" Maneuver. *You think that if you don't think God will intervene, He probably won't.* Galatians 6:7–10; Philippians 2:12–13.

5. The "No Fire Now Means No Fire Later" Gamble. *You believe that if God doesn't discipline you immediately when you sin, He won't do anything later, either.* Romans 2:4–11; 1 Corinthians 11:31–32; 2 Peter 3:1–9.

Lying on my bed that afternoon, I finally submitted to His discipline. In tearful repentance, I confessed my sin, not only of stealing but also of stubbornly-held attitudes of rebellion and compromise. I recommitted myself to doing the right thing, no matter what the cost. The next morning, I walked up to a very surprised store manager, handed him his dollars along with my apology, and walked out of there a very relieved and renewed woman!

You are drenched with peace when you say yes to your Father, the Vinedresser!

Imagine yourself standing in a cool, clear forest pool. Your arms are open wide. Your face is up. Your eyes are closed. A pure, cool waterfall is splashing over you and around you . . . and you are drenched with peace.

That's how it feels when you say yes to your Father, the Vinedresser, as He washes away the sin that's covering your life!

I invite you right now to quiet your heart before the Lord. Ask Him if there is anything in your life that is grieving Him. Then be still before Him for the next sixty seconds.

It might be the longest minute you've experienced in a long time, but if you say yes to whatever God is asking you to do, it will be the best sixty seconds, too!

Now let's return to the vineyard and discover God's surprising plan to prepare you and me—not just to have *some* spiritual fruit in our lives, but *more* fruit.

Much more!

"Every branch that
bears fruit He prunes, that it
may bear more fruit."

JOHN 15:2

CHAPTER FOUR

Making Room for More

The truckloads of baskets arrived before dawn. The woman and her father were out early to make sure that baskets were deposited at each row, ready for the pickers to begin the day's work.

This was the first day of harvest: the day that the calendar of vineyard life rushed toward, the day when the results of work done months before would become apparent for everyone to see. Fortunately, the weather had turned mild and dry—perfect for protecting the ripe fruit from damage or mold.

The hours passed in a flurry of picking, carrying overflowing baskets to the truck, and driving the loads of harvested grapes to town. For the next several weeks, the busy scene in the vineyard would be repeated until the last grape was picked.

Late in the afternoon, when the pickers had gone home, the young woman sat in the shade of an arbor with her father. Their hands were stained, their backs were tired—and they were both elated. Every sign pointed to an exceptional year.

"Papa," she began, "even the older men were remarking today about your grapes. They can't remember picking such stunning fruit. I heard them shouting 'Bellisimo! Bellisimo!' all over the vineyard!"

"Umm," he responded contentedly, his eyes half-closed.

"They say all of Tuscany will remember this harvest," she continued. "When I went with the trucks to town today, everyone there wanted to know your secret."

"And what did you tell them?"

"I told them what you always say." She turned playfully to face him, then recited, "The secret of taking more to town in September is leaving more behind all year long."

"What an excellent student you are, my dear!" he exclaimed. "But did they understand?"

"Some," she mused. "But not many."

———————

The vinedresser in our story understood and applied the wonderful principle of "leaving more behind." If you're a home gardener, I imagine you do, too. Early every spring you pay special attention to your dwarf apple trees or your prize rose bushes. Why? Because you know that the size and condition of the fruit or flowers you hope to enjoy later in the year will depend on what you do now.

And what you have to do now is prune.

One gardening manual in our house defines pruning as "removing unwanted plant parts for a purpose." You cut away unnecessary shoots. You pinch back buds and foliage to redirect growth. Your purpose is more fruit or bigger blooms.

Pruning is God's way of making room in your life for more of what matters most.

The same is true in our spiritual lives. Jesus shared a second powerful secret of the vine that night in the vineyard when He said, "Every branch that bears fruit He prunes, that it may bear more fruit" (v. 2).

Clearly, Jesus wanted you and me to understand what God, in His great love for us, does to increase our fruitfulness.

The whole idea of spiritual pruning tells us that we have to let go of a lot of our "pretty good" to receive God's very best. This surprising truth is at the heart of the second secret of the vine.

> ## Second Secret of the Vine:
>
> *If your life bears some fruit,*
> *God will intervene to prune you . . .*
> *so that you will bear more fruit.*

In a grape plant, pruning redirects the sap away from wasteful growth and toward desirable fruit. In our lives, pruning is God's way of making room for more of what matters most, and redirecting the flow of His life through us so that we'll produce more of what will last for eternity.

Even though being pruned isn't much fun, the purpose for it is full of promise. In fact, if you cooperate with God's shears, you'll soon find yourself shaking your head—not over what you have left behind, but at the wonderful new results you see flourishing all around.

The Trouble with Leaves

Think of leaves as those activities, preoccupations, and priorities that, though not wrong, are using up valuable resources that would be better spent in pursuit of fruitfulness for God.

I don't know about you, but I'm especially skilled at producing an abundance of "leaves" in my life! As women, we enjoy creating an attractive, comfortable life for those we love. But we can get so caught up in the demands of the immediate that we leave no room for the future God is trying to give us.

For my friend Gail, teaching a weekly Bible study in her home had for years been a fulfilling and fruitful activity. For some time, though, busyness had kept her from taking the next step—one that was wide open to her—of developing a video teaching curriculum that would reach many

She had been busy doing good. But God was inviting her to reach for His best.

more with the same material. Last year she finally took a step of faith. She reprioritized her activities, turned her group over to a woman she had been mentoring, and headed for the recording studio.

"I always prayed that God would use me to teach more women," she told me, "but I wanted to do it my way. Giving up certain activities was difficult. But already God is using the video teaching to reach thousands of women I could never touch personally."

As God begins to prune in your life, your first reaction may be to wail, "What have I done wrong?" But the truth is that if God is pruning you, you're doing something right!

You're not bogged down in ongoing, serious sin. You're already busy bearing fruit. But your loving Father wants to help you bear "more fruit" for His glory.

Was Gail doing something wrong? Of course not. She had been busy doing good. But God was inviting her to do more—to reach for His best.

God doesn't prune away sin—that's what He does with His discipline. His pruning focuses on the second-

DISCIPLINE VERSUS PRUNING: A COMPARISON		
ISSUE	DISCIPLINING	PRUNING
HOW DO YOU KNOW IT'S HAPPENING?	Pain	Discomfort
WHY IS IT HAPPENING?	You're doing something wrong (sin)	You're doing something right (bearing fruit)
WHAT IS YOUR LEVEL OF FRUITFULNESS?	No fruit	Fruit
WHAT IS THE VINEDRESSER'S DESIRE?	Fruit	More fruit
WHAT NEEDS TO GO?	Sin (disobeying the Lord)	Self (putting myself before God)
HOW SHOULD YOU FEEL?	Guilty, sad	Relief, trust
WHAT IS THE RIGHT RESPONSE?	Repentance (stop your sin)	Release (surrender to God)
WHEN DOES IT STOP?	When you stop your sin	When God is finished

best pursuits that can take over our lives, or on values or activities that used to be a priority for us but shouldn't be any longer. They can waste our potential for weeks or months. Maybe even for a lifetime.

What God's Shears Look Like

Of course, God doesn't come marching into your kitchen brandishing an enormous pair of pruning shears! So how does He work?

As we'll see, God prunes people indirectly. He works through His people and our key relationships. He speaks to us through His Word. He nudges us through the press of challenging circumstances—perhaps trials at home, on the job, or in our finances. He leads by the insistent voice of His Spirit in our hearts.

However God chooses to work, He will get our attention, creating discomfort if necessary, so that we can focus on and respond to the point of His pruning.

Since every branch in Christ gets pruned, we know that the Vinedresser is at work everywhere in the family of God right now—including your life and mine! Having spent years talking to women on this subject, I've noticed a recurring pattern of focal points for God's pruning shears:

- Priorities that need to be rearranged
- Relationships that need to change or end
- Busyness that isn't accomplishing what matters most
- Dependencies or attachments that we're ready to grow out of
- Personal "rights" that God is asking us to surrender to Him

Where do you think God might be pruning in your life today?

If you have no idea, try this: Look for recurring pressure points (you could call them "invitations") in your reading of God's Word, your conversations with your spiritual mentors, the challenges you've faced recently. Tell God you're ready to acknowledge His will and surrender with an open heart.

SHEAR AMAZEMENT: STORIES OF LIFE AFTER PRUNING

George Mueller wrote, "Our Father never takes anything from his children unless he means to give them something better." Do you believe that? I do! And so do the women you're about to meet. They have responded to the Vinedresser's pruning, too, and discovered God's "something better."

Donna: "Fixing Brad was not my personal responsibility."

Donna admits she was constantly trying to get her husband, Brad, to read his Bible and be more spiritual. One day, Brad picked up the latest Christian book she had handed him and threw it across the room. "If you don't stop nagging me," he announced angrily, "I'll walk out that door and never come back!" Frightened and heartsick, Donna asked God what to do.

"I was able to share my heart with these women because I knew how it felt to have nothing."

"The following months were intensely painful as God went to work in my heart," she recalls. A friend helped her see that it was not her job to make Brad holy. "I realized that my worry and well-intentioned meddling were getting in God's way," she says. When she let God change her attitudes and actions, things changed with Brad, too. Says Donna, "There is more harmony in our marriage and more spiritual openness today than I ever could have accomplished my way."

Janis: "Our home and all our possessions are always on loan."

Janis and her husband had been married for twenty-five years when through an act of arson their home burned to the ground. "Everything we owned was gone," she says. "It took only days, through the kindness of friends and family, to begin a new home, but it took months for me to let go emotionally of all I had lost. I wept every time I remembered a baby photo album or a gift from one of my children."

Eventually, Janis saw that even though the Lord mourned her loss with her, He was inviting her to grow from it. She volunteered for a program at her church to help homeless women. "I was able to genuinely share my heart with these women because I knew how it felt to have nothing. I came to realize that God used this tragedy as a surprise opportunity for pruning."

With him gone, she spent most evenings idly watching television or brooding.

Today, Janis and her husband serve as missionaries. She says, "Without learning that my possessions are on loan from God, I could never have left everything to serve Him overseas. But what we're seeing now is fruit that will last forever. And we've never been happier!"

Margie: "My illness was not a mistake."

Tall, striking, and outgoing, Margie was a born leader who was busy using her gifts for God. But one day, Margie became ill and had to be hospitalized. After an operation, the surgeon announced that she would have to feed herself through a tube inserted into her stomach for the rest of her life.

"Month after month I sought the Lord for healing to be able to return to my work for Him," she recalls. For three years, Margie suffered with her debilitating condition, and then one day God miraculously healed her. The stomach tube was removed, she regained her strength, and gradually she began to minister again. But Margie was an amazingly different person. In fact, her work with others has been dramatically more effective because of her increased sensitivity and compassion.

> *For years God has been asking for me to surrender my expectations to Him.*

"I learned that while God has plans for our gifts and abilities, He can have even greater plans for our desperate need of Him," she says now. "I believe God pruned me through my illness so that I could relate better to the daily struggles of others. That's where real ministry begins anyway."

Mavis: "I let God peel my fingers off my husband's job."

Mavis had been praying for years that God would bring her husband Ed a job that would allow him to be at home every evening. With him gone, she spent most evenings idly watching television or brooding.

"I was miserable until I let God peel my fingers off what I wanted and accepted the opportunities He had been trying to give me—time with my kids, time to encourage single moms we know, time to seek Him," she says. "The quality of our family life has changed completely."

Mavis is still praying for a different job for Ed. But she has taken a huge step forward in maturity and impact for God.

Sandy: "My perfect voice was not the voice others could hear best."

A gifted young singer, Sandy loved serving the Lord with her voice. Then she developed a lump in her throat. When surgery left her with damaged vocal cords, Sandy was devastated. She couldn't understand why her greatest gift had been taken from her.

For two years, Sandy continued to write songs but refused to sing. One Sunday, as a favor to her husband, she sang his favorite song during the evening service. A visitor, who happened to be the president of a recording company, was so moved by the emotional power of her singing that he offered Sandy a contract. Her CD is now being distributed through a mission organization to churches around the world.

"God took away my 'perfect' voice," Sandy says, "and gave me a voice that would reach more people in deeper ways for Him."

Nora: "I decided to give up my 'right' to be married."

Ever since she had become a believer, Nora felt she had a "right" to be married. In the past, this attitude had led her into destructive relationships with non-Christian men. Even though she had put an end to those, Nora still held tightly to her belief that God owed her a husband.

Pruning always involves surrender and relinquishment on our part.

"As I learned about the principle of pruning, I saw that for years God has been asking for me to surrender my expectations to Him," she says. One night she tearfully relinquished a long list of "rights"—to be married, to be in control, to be thin. "Most of all," she says, "my 'right' to continually mourn the mistakes I have made in the past."

"I can't describe the peace I now have," Nora says. "When anxiety begins to arise over 'What do I do now?' I simply give the Lord my 'right' to worry. These days, I'm enjoying much healthier relationships with others, and the blessed assurance that the Lord has always known what is best for me. Of course, being the perfect gentleman that He is, He has never forced His best on me!"

WITH OPEN HANDS

As you've listened to these women's stories, what has the Lord brought to your mind? You might have realized that in your life, the Vinedresser has been pruning you in an important area that is unique to you. He may be asking you to say yes to His hand in your finances, your desire to be comfortable or secure, a family situation, or a new season of your life.

I didn't understand that every gift in this life has a time limit.

Pruning always involves surrender and relinquishment on our part. God asks us to keep our hands open to His ways and His will. He may ask us to let go of something that feels important to our happiness. No wonder we feel discomfort or even pain in pruning! Yet we know from James 1:17 that "every good gift and every perfect gift is from above, and comes down from the Father." So my encouragement to you is to receive His pruning as nothing less than an unexpected, unasked-for, but exceedingly precious gift! Because that's what pruning is. As, George McDonald wrote, "God's fingers can touch nothing except to mold it into loveliness."

Here's something I've learned about God's gifts that has meant a great deal to me:

I grew up believing that everything I love, treasure, enjoy, and consider good on earth is a gift from God. But I didn't understand that every gift in this life has a time limit. People die, possessions can be destroyed, and positions taken away. That's just the way life is. And if I assume that everything I hold in my hand today is mine to keep, I will be deeply disappointed. Ultimately, I'll begin to question God's character and His intentions toward me—and that can spell big trouble.

Pruning means we lose something now to gain something later.

So besides keeping my hands open, I've imagined a place for an expiration date written on the back of each treasure in my life. Then I leave it up to God to fill in that date. Why not? He is the only one who knows my future anyway. And He is the only one who knows what would be best for me. As David wrote:

> But as for me, I trust in You, O LORD;
>   I say, "You are my God."
> My times are in Your hand.

PSALM 31:14–15

Cutting Loose from Pruning Tangles
adapted from *Secrets of the Vine Bible Study*

If you recognize yourself in any of the false beliefs below, let God's Word prepare you to receive the work of abundance He wants for your life. Then write out your new breakthrough belief in your journal.

1. You think, "God is picking on me unfairly." 2 Corinthians 1:3–7; Hebrews 5:8–9; James 1:2–12; 1 Peter 1:6–7.

2. You assume, "God has abandoned me." Psalm 23; Psalm 139:1–6; Daniel 3:15–18; John 14:18; Romans 8:35–39.

3. You exclaim, "God is asking too much!" Genesis 50:19–20; Job 23:8–10; 2 Corinthians 9:8.

4. You wonder, "Does God really know what's going on?" Isaiah 55:8–9; Matthew 6:8, 25–34; Romans 11:33–36.

5. You reason, "How could a loving God allow this to happen?" Psalm 73; Romans 8:28, 37–39; 2 Corinthians 12:7–10.

The truth is that you cannot determine or control how long you will have your husband, your children, your parents, your job, your home, or your health. If you'll release your emotional ownership of these things, you'll respond much more positively when the time comes to release back to Him what He so lovingly and willingly loaned you in the first place. And you'll be much more able to receive His comfort in your loss as well as thank Him for the time you had to enjoy His gifts.

FRUIT IN DUE SEASON

I'll admit, it would be wonderful if we could see the fruit to come while the pruning is happening. But that's not how life in the vineyard works. Fruit takes time to mature. Pruning means we lose something now to gain something later—something we probably could never see or imagine at the moment.

That's why the Vinedresser invites us to trust Him. If you're in the middle of a painful pruning season right now, you may not even have the emotional energy to think, much less be grateful for what God is doing. But please know that our Father is patient and kind. He

You can pour out your heart and know that He cares—about your tomorrow and your today.

knows your heart, and His heart is broken with yours, too. Remember that He is the One who "heals the brokenhearted and binds up their wounds" (Psalm 147:3). His name is "the Father of mercies and God of all comfort" (2 Corinthians 1:3). You can pour out your heart and know that He cares—about your tomorrow and your today. His skillful hand is at work in your life accomplishing something in you that you could not do for yourself.

You'll be bearing more fruit for God—by your prayers, your choice to give thanks, and your daily actions before others.

Make room in your heart for that miracle today. Give God the time He needs to accomplish something large and enduring and beautiful in your life for Him.

Whatever you do, don't let your resistance to God's pruning trip you into anger and rebellion. That will only send you back into a season of discipline—and God wants that even less for you than you do!

Instead, receive the gift from the Vinedresser's hand today and look forward, with confidence and anticipation, to the season of "more fruit" that is just around the corner. As soon as you do, you'll already be bearing more fruit for God—by your prayers, your choice to give thanks, and your daily actions before others. They'll see God's goodness affirmed by what you do and say in the midst of your circumstances. Your faith will plant the seeds of faith in them. They'll be encouraged, and God will be pleased and glorified.

*"He who abides in Me,
and I in him, bears much fruit."*

<small>JOHN 15:5</small>

CHAPTER FIVE

The Miracle of Much Fruit

On the final day of harvest, the vineyard held its annual prize branch competition. The contest was based on a question the vinedresser had put to his workers when they first arrived: "Which single branch in my vineyard do you think will yield the most grapes?"

This year's results were astonishing. Entrants brought in heavier baskets than ever before. And the winner, to everyone's surprise, was a first-year worker—a young boy from Siena. He hauled in twenty more pounds of fruit from his one branch than the next closest contestant.

The young woman, at least, was suspicious.

"Papa," she asked as the last worker was departing, "how did that boy know which branch would win the prize?"

"He has a good memory."

"What do you mean?" she said.

"When he came here last winter to ask for a job, we walked

through the rows together." Her father winked. "I showed him which branch would win this year."

The daughter gasped in disbelief. "But how could you do that? The branches then were still completely bare!"

"Yes, but that's when you can see the place that will tell." He paused.

She waited, wanting him to say more, to explain what exactly he meant by the place that will tell.

"Come, I'll show you," her father said finally. They walked to a nearby row. "Look," he said, pointing to the place where a branch and vine met. "You measure the circumference of the branch here—do you see?—right where it comes out of the trunk."

Yes, she did see. The branch her father pointed to grew thick and strong out of the vine. She noticed that another branch nearby was only a quarter as big around at the same place.

Her father continued. "The size of this meeting place reveals the potential size of the harvest to come. The harvest cannot be greater than this union allows. It would be impossible! On the other hand, the greater this union, the greater can be the yield."

They looked over the rows of branches, clean-picked now until the next season. "And do you have more secrets that would win me a prize?" she asked.

"Perhaps," he said with a smile. "But none better."

The biggest miracle in any vineyard is an unseen one. It flows like a silent river beneath the rough bark of the grape plant. It surges up through the trunk of the vine, out into the branches, and from there to the clusters of swelling fruit.

That unseen miracle is sap—the lifeblood of any vineyard. And as the vinedresser in our story knew, the greater the connection between branch and vine, the more lifeblood is available to produce fruit.

Of course, the power of sap to make an abundance of fruit matters most in a branch that is healthy (that isn't being dragged down by dirt and disease) and well-pruned (that isn't sending its nutrients in a dozen competing directions). Only then can the flow of life through the connecting place of vine to branch bring results that are truly miraculous.

Jesus' name for that mysterious and powerful connection is abiding. He said:

> *"He who abides in Me, and I in him, bears much fruit."*
>
> JOHN 15:5

What does Jesus mean by "abide"? It's not a word we use much these days, but the concept is simple. It means to stay, to remain, to continue in fellowship with. In that word, Jesus was calling His disciples to strengthen and enlarge their connection to Him, the Vine—to *be with Him* more and more.

And the direct result of such intimacy, Jesus promised, would be *"much fruit."*

If you think about the circumstances of that conversation in the vineyard, you can almost taste the anguish and the longing. After all, Jesus had just told His best friends that He was leaving. Physically, they would *not* be together! Yet He pleaded with them, *"Abide in Me, and I in you."* Within just six verses in John 15, you'll find that Jesus repeated His appeal to "abide" ten times!

You don't have to wait until you become more mature, more successful, or more accepted.

So the first thing I want you to grasp in this chapter is just how much the Lord Jesus *wants* to abide with you. The Creator of the Universe, the perfect Son of God, the Savior of your soul wants to be in a continuing, growing, thriving, and incredibly productive relationship . . . with *you.*

You don't have to know more in order to abide. You don't have to wait until you become more mature, more successful, or more accepted. You don't have to prove yourself in any way more worthy. Right now, as you read this page, you are already the object of your Lord's attention and affection.

>*Stay with Me,* He says.
>*Be with Me.*
>*Remain in Me.*

Are you ready to hear that amazing invitation in a fresh way today? Then you may be ready to make a breakthrough to the most abundant life possible. And you'll find it in the third and final secret of the vine.

THE THIRD SECRET OF THE VINE:

*If your life bears more fruit,
God will invite you to abide more deeply
with Him because that's how He produces
much fruit through you.*

You might be as relieved as I was to learn that you don't reach your spiritual potential by cramming more serving or doing for God into your day! In fact, the opposite is true.

It's only as you pursue genuine and unbroken intimacy with Him that you can produce the most eternal fruit for His glory.

And that should be good news for any woman.

THE LANGUAGE OF WOMEN

Surely this last secret—abiding—is especially meaningful for us. Jesus is talking our language here, don't you think? It is the language of relationship, of mutual enjoyment, of personal connectedness. God seems to have gifted women with a special passion for closeness, both with those we love and with our Lord. Compared to the average male, most women I know seem to express their emotions more readily, enjoy fellowship more naturally, and desire togetherness more enthusiastically.

Can't you just feel the tension mounting in that little house?

But there's a catch.

God also seemed to wire us to care and tend and please more instinctively, too. And that often adds up to out-of-control demands and dawn-till-dusk busyness.

That's why abiding isn't automatic, even for us. We must choose, usually in the face of intense pressures, to heed the urgent call of Jesus to come away and "be with Me."

The familiar story of sisters Mary and Martha memorably portrays these competing priorities in our lives (Luke 10:38–42). When Jesus and His disciples stopped at their home in Bethany one day, "Mary . . . sat at Jesus' feet and heard His word. But Martha was distracted with much serving" (vv. 39–40).

Can't you just feel the tension mounting in that little house? Will it be *relationship* or will it be *service* that wins the day? Two sisters want to know!

Finally, a very agitated Martha asked Jesus to tell her sister to get up and start helping. But Jesus gave a tender and surprising reply:

> *"Martha, Martha, you are worried and troubled about many things. But one thing is needed, and Mary has chosen that good part."*
>
> vv. 41–42

Martha made the perfectly responsible "ministry" choice (I'm pretty sure I would have, too). She threw her energies and skills into making sure everything was going well and everyone was cared for. But Mary chose to abide with Jesus. And when Martha asked Jesus to rebuke her sister for not caring enough to serve Him, Jesus declined. Why? Because Mary had chosen to *be with Him,* and that was better than *doing for Him.*

Often I start my day as Mary. "Come be with Me," I hear the Lord saying. "In a moment, Lord," I reply. "But first I need to get a load of wash started, and Jessica ready, and I need to be out the door at . . ." Before I know it, the demands of the day have swept me away, worried and troubled about many things, and my name is Martha.

I sensed God asking me to spend the hour simply enjoying His presence.

Does this sound familiar to you? Most women I know struggle to get to the end of their to-do list each day. Spending time with God becomes just another activity on our list, when in fact it should be the paper on which we prioritize everything else we do!

God asks us to choose to abide, but look what happens when we don't. Jesus said:

> *"He who abides in Me, and I in him, bears much fruit; for without Me you can do nothing."*
>
> JOHN 15:5

Nothing? You and I tend to think that the only way to get more out of our day is to cram more into it. But the message of Jesus for us Martha's of the world is clear: *You're too busy not to abide!*

TOO BUSY *Not* TO ABIDE

I happen to be a fairly organized person, and I enjoy being well prepared. For years I taught a monthly Bible study class, spending hours preparing my lessons and typing up handouts. But one month, a series of unexpected events kept me so busy that I couldn't prepare. The morning of class I finally got an hour to myself, but by then I was desperate. I knelt next to my bed and cried out to the Lord for His help. How did He want me to use that time?

I walked into class feeling stripped of the very things that usually gave me confidence.

Strangely, I sensed God asking me to spend the hour simply enjoying His presence. So I took courage and stayed on my knees until it was time to go.

I walked into class feeling stripped of the very things that usually gave me confidence—organization, tools, a detailed plan. Since the normal schedule for class was out of the question, I opened in prayer, then turned to a favorite passage. From those treasured words, I talked about what

God had taught me over the years on that subject. As unplanned as the presentation was, not once during the lesson did I doubt that God was in it. I noticed women leaning forward listening, soaking up what was being shared. By the end of class, several were in tears. One woman wanted to know how I knew that my topic was the very issue she had been asking God to help her with.

The busier we are, the more we need to abide.

As I drove home, I understood for the first time how doing less *for* God and being more *with* God produced *much* fruit. Now for you, that truth may seem obvious. But if you're one of my detail-oriented, super-organized sisters, I know you can understand what a breakthrough that was for me.

Let me share something else. The more experience we have in ministry, the easier it is to coast along on our talents, our store of knowledge, our experience, and our well-developed teaching aids . . . and leave God more and more out of the picture. Of course that's not our intention. But without being aware of it, we can forget that to do God's work, we need God's presence and power—and more of it all the time! In His invitation to abide, Jesus asks us to become more and more *dependent* on Him, and the amazing result is an abundance of fruit.

Think about it. Real and lasting fruit doesn't happen when you and I are not deeply connected to Jesus any more than a branch can bear fruit if it is lying on the ground. Jesus said:

> *"As the branch cannot bear fruit of itself,*
> *unless it abides in the vine, neither can you,*
> *unless you abide in Me."*
>
> v. 4

In fact, the busier we are, the more we need to abide. Because abiding is precisely how we are refueled and can avoid emotional and spiritual burnout.

So how does it work? And what do we have to do to abide?

That depends on who you are…

Every pilgrim travels toward God with a promise in hand—we can know God.

TOOLS TO ABIDING

Just as you relate to and communicate with each of your children differently, God invites each of us to abide with Him in our unique way. Yet all through Scripture and for thousands of years, the road to intimacy with God has had the same guideposts.

Being a pilgrim still requires humility, perseverance, obedience, and a genuine desire to know the Lord in a more personal way.

And every pilgrim travels toward God with a promise in hand—we *can* know God. "Draw near to God and He will draw near to you," the Bible says (James 4:8). "You will seek Me and find Me, when you search for Me with all your heart" (Jeremiah 29:13).

With this in mind, here are some suggestions that will help you begin or continue to abide.

My prayer seemed to go on forever. But when I opened my eyes, only five minutes had passed.

1. Make an appointment.

One morning while I was playing with my grandson, the doorbell rang. Jonathan was just a year old, so I picked him up and carried him to the door. The visitor was my neighbor dropping off a letter that had been left in her mailbox by mistake.

After we had chatted for several minutes, Jonathan put his little hands on each side of my face and turned it toward his. As I looked into his eyes, I realized he was saying, "Grandmother, I want all your attention."

That's what God wants from you. But that's difficult to

do unless you make a plan to abide, and make that plan a *priority*. Choose a time when you are at your best. Decide on a quiet and private place. Then make an appointment, write it down, and post it somewhere you can see it.

Keep it as regularly as you can. If you miss, apologize (just as you'd treat any best friend), and receive His forgiveness gratefully and confidently.

2. Read and meditate on God's Letter to you.

As a new Christian, reading my Bible was a spiritual discipline that helped me know what the Bible said and how God wanted me to live. But as I have grown in my faith, I have wanted more. I want to hear God's Word speaking directly into my life about pressing circumstances. More and more, I desire to have a personal encounter with Jesus on the pages of Scripture.

I believe this is what Jesus had in mind when He said, "Abide in Me." He wasn't advising His disciples to learn more about Jewish history or law; they already knew a lot about that. He was asking for an ongoing, personal encounter. Therefore, in your abiding time, I encourage you to read the Bible as God's letter to you. Let His words remain in you. Contemplate them. Take them with you from the room. Paul said, "Let the word of Christ dwell in you richly" (Colossians 3:16). And as you do, His words to you will begin to transform your thoughts and feelings and values.

3. Talk to God.

I remember the first time I determined to get up early and spend thirty minutes praying. It seemed simple enough. So I got down on my knees and prayed. I prayed for all my concerns, for everyone I could think of, and for everything around the world. My prayer seemed to go on forever. But when I opened my eyes, only five minutes had passed. *How do "spiritual" people pray for a whole hour?* I wondered.

The answer, I discovered, is that prayer is not a monologue, but a conversation with a friend. People who pray well talk to God well—as if He is there and listening and deeply involved, which He truly is.

It is helpful to have a list of people and situations that you pray for regularly (some things come up all the time between you and your other close friends, too). But because you're abiding with God Himself, you can also pour out your deepest fears, your hidden feelings, and your honest thoughts to Him. And of course, close friends also make a point of expressing their affection and gratitude often.

4. Keep a spiritual journal.

Write a letter to God each day in a notebook. This is not a diary of your day (although you may include some of that), but rather a record of how you are doing spiritually. Write down what God is teaching you. Record the Scriptures that mean the most to you. Write your prayers, and keep track of the answers. Ask and expect God to show you His heart, even as you write.

Don't give a second thought to how well you write or spell. Even the psalmist David knew, "Before a word is on my tongue you know it completely, O LORD" (Psalm 139:4, NIV). Your spiritual journal is private and personal. Go back to it often to see what God is doing in your life, and how you're changing.

5. Practice unbroken abiding.

Is it possible for a busy woman to be aware of God's presence every moment of every day—while you drive, shop, work, or even converse with another person? Everything else would be what you did *while* you were abiding with Christ.

The truth is that it *is* possible. Paul referred to it as "praying without ceasing." Brother Lawrence, a lay minister who spent years working in a monastery kitchen, called it "practicing the presence of God." It's easy for us to think of abiding as an event that ends when our quiet time ends. Then we go on with the real business of our day. But communing with the Lord is more like an ongoing attentiveness to the One who is *always* abiding with us. And we can do that anywhere.

A friend of mine describes unbroken abiding like this: "It's a silent conversation going on inside myself. But instead of thinking or talking to myself, I direct my thoughts toward God. He's always included. I'm learning to have a running conversation with Him no matter what I'm doing. My relationship has gone from a date I had with God in the morning to an all-day love affair in His presence."

MY FIRST SOURCE

When you and I are deeply in touch with the source of all life, our lives change. Most of all, *we* change in important ways—and in very down-to-earth ways, too. Take your marriage or other primary relationships, for example.

I'll never forget how startled I was the day my new husband blurted out in some frustration, "It's not my job to make you happy."

"Then whose job is it?" I asked. But even before the words were out of my mouth I knew the answer. And it certainly wasn't my husband.

I'll admit that as a young wife I assumed that Bruce would be the ultimate source of fulfillment and happiness in my life (just like all the love songs promise). Yes, I loved God, and I wanted to grow in my faith. But the relationship I abided in most was with Bruce. That meant I looked to Bruce for the kind of intimacy that would make me feel whole, significant, and content. When Bruce failed to deliver at this impossible task, I could become desperate and demanding.

You will tend to ask for the very things that are His will and delight to give.

Does this pattern sound familiar to you? When a woman makes someone other than Jesus the ultimate source of her contentment, she ends up taxing others unreasonably, asking them to meet spiritual and emotional needs that can only be met by God. The results can be painful and disillusioning.

God may proactively prune us in this area, causing others to *withhold* what we want from them because He wants us to receive it from Him. Remember that our God describes Himself as a jealous God (Exodus 34:14). He asks to be our first affection, our first provider, our first security.

Perhaps you haven't heard the "jealousy" in these words from Jesus to you about abiding:

> *"As the Father loved Me, I also have loved you; abide in My love."*
> JOHN 15:9

As you abide in this wonderful, attentive, and fulfilling love of God, you can expect other relationships in your life to improve dramatically! They don't have to fill you up—God does. They don't have to explain and sustain your existence—God does. I don't mean that human relationships will lose their importance in your life. But instead of allowing your needs to define and limit those relationships, you will more often come to them brimming with the love of God, ready to give freely from the river of abundance that flows from His heart through yours.

Let me show you in more detail how that will happen.

GRAPE EXPECTATIONS

The power of abiding in a woman's life will change you from the inside out:

You will become more like Christ.

As you spend more and more time being with Him, you'll notice the character of Jesus being developed in you. It's a fact that the more time you spend with a person, the more you take on their traits. Spend time in the gospels and make a list of some of the qualities of Jesus you would like to be true of you. Then watch God produce them in you as you abide in Him more frequently.

You will gain wisdom and discernment.

The more time you spend with God, the more you'll grow in godly discernment. God wants you to know His will, and He will give you wisdom as you wait patiently on Him (James 1:5).

When you need to make an important decision—abide. God will faithfully direct you as you spend time in His presence. When you are struggling with a relationship—abide. When you are uncertain about whether you are being pruned or disciplined—abide. God will be faithful to reveal the truth to you.

You will pray more in keeping with God's will—and He will answer.

Jesus said, "If you abide in Me, and My words abide in you, you will ask what you desire, and it shall be done for you" (John 15:7). What an astonishing promise! Yet it makes sense. When you are abiding deeply in Jesus, your heart and mind become much more attuned to Him and His purposes. As a result, you will tend to ask for the very things that are His will and delight to give.

You will experience His peace and presence.

The more time you spend with Christ, the more you will experience the peace of His presence even in the midst of trials and crisis. A friend of mine recently found herself caught in the middle of a robbery in progress. She was tempted to run for the exit sign, but clearly sensed God saying, "Don't run!"

He wants the pleasure of your company—anytime, anywhere, anyhow.

"After the ordeal was over," she says, "I realized that I had been calm throughout it. And had I run for the door, I may have been shot. I believe I heard God because my heart was at peace, and that has come from the disciplines of abiding in my life. I'm learning to believe that safety doesn't exist in the absence of danger, but in the presence of God."

And besides all this, the practice of abiding will bring you a special and very personal gift from Jesus. He called it "My joy."

Five Abiding Busters

adapted from *Secrets of the Vine Bible Study*

See if you recognize yourself in the "abiding busters" on this page (each example, while powerful, is wrong). Let the Bible help you discover a new breakthrough truth, and write it down (in your own words) in your journal.

1. The "But I Don't Feel Anything" Foul-Up. *You assume if you didn't have strong emotions, nothing happened.* Psalm 145:18; 1 John 3:19–20.

2. The "He Doesn't Like Me" Muddle. *You believe God loves you, but you doubt that He actually likes you.* John 15:15; Ephesians 3:17–19; 1 John 3:1.

3. The "I'm Too Busy" Blunder. *You let your schedule keep you from regular abiding, but you think God will connect with you anyway.* Isaiah 40:31; Matthew 6:33; Matthew 11:28.

4. The "Sin Doesn't Matter" Mistake. *You think ongoing disobedience won't keep you from abiding, especially if you experience pleasant feelings during church.* Psalm 15; Psalm 66:18–20; James 4:8; 1 John 1:5-7.

5. The "Going Through the Motions" Notion. *You think Bible reading and prayer are proof you're having a relationship with God.* 1 Samuel 16:7; Psalm 27:4–8; Matthew 5:6.

AN INVITATION TO JOY

Joy, you see, was ultimately the very reason Jesus gave for His message in the vineyard. He said so Himself:

> *"These things I have spoken to you, that My joy may remain in you, and that your joy may be full."*
>
> V. 11

You might be a mother of a newborn who has you up all hours of the night. You might be caring almost hourly for an elderly and ailing parent. You might feel completely unable or unworthy to sit at Jesus' feet.

If you say yes, He will give you His joy.

Jesus wants you to know the truth today. He wants the pleasure of your company—anytime, anywhere, anyhow—and if you say yes, He will give you His joy.

I hope that these past few chapters have stirred in you an increasing desire for extraordinary fruitfulness for God. In our next and final chapter, we're going to ask some key questions about your relationship with your Father. Together, we'll uncover potential barriers that would keep you from experiencing all He has in mind for your life.

Remember, what God has in mind for you is so far beyond what you are experiencing right now that you can't possibly imagine it. You—one magnificent branch in the Father's vineyard—were made for abundance.

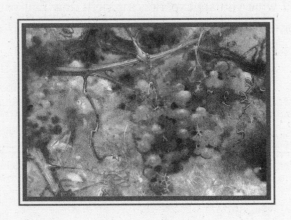

*He who has begun
a good work in you will complete it
until the day of Jesus Christ.*

PHILIPPIANS 1:6

CHAPTER SIX

Your Father's Prize

She sat by the window of the train watching the red tile roofs, hilltop villages, and neatly tended vineyards of Tuscany slip past. Siena, Empoli, Pontedera . . . the valley towns of her childhood memory came and went. Soon the train would turn north, taking her away from Italy and back to her life in the city.

Suddenly she remembered her father's parting gift. She pulled the little package from her coat pocket, and when she opened it, an oval silver locket fell into her lap.

She examined it, delighted. On its cover, the locket showed an embossing of a grape cluster. Inside it held a sepia photograph. The picture showed her as a small girl sitting astride her father's broad shoulders as he stood proudly beside a row of his beloved grapes.

On the facing frame she read in tiny script, "You will always be my greatest prize. Love, Papa."

At that moment, a thought occurred to her. Why it hadn't before, she couldn't say. What she saw for the first time was that her father's prize-winning ways with a vineyard were like a picture of how he had always cared for her.

Gazing out the window, she thought about his dedication to a lifetime of coaxing a harvest from his grapes. And how, with an even greater dedication, he had coaxed an abundance of the heart from her life—gently correcting her when necessary, firmly guiding her toward maturity, and consistently proving his unconditional love.

As the train clattered toward the border, her future seemed to rush toward her, faster and faster. But the future she saw was full of promise. Her father had prepared her for whatever lay ahead. And holding the picture of it tightly in her hands, she basked in the glow of joyful anticipation.

I trust that our time in the vineyard together has been a refreshing and encouraging experience for you. My prayer is that, as you leave these pages, you'll take with you a new portrait of your heavenly Father's love, along with a deeper desire to cooperate with His ways in your life.

Jesus said, "My Father is always at his work . . . and I, too, am working" (John 5:17, NIV). Isn't that amazing? God Himself is at work—always—in every circumstance of our life, and in every challenge we face!

And how kind it is of Jesus to give us such a memorable illustration of this miracle! A vine. A branch full of promise. A Vinedresser, always at work. A plan for a huge harvest from every disciple . . .

Yet the truth is that many women do not reach for the promise. They hesitate here, at the threshold of spiritual and emotional abundance. Why? Sooner or later, it seems to me, the issue reveals itself to be a relational one—a basic question of trust between daughter and Father.

I think of a Vermont woman named Maeve. After reading *Secrets of the Vine,* she called it a "volume of hope." It had helped her to resolve a long-standing break in her relationship with her Father. "I always felt like God's stepdaughter," she wrote. "Even though I was saved at eighteen, I have often felt emotionally destitute. Personal challenges in my life and years of physical suffering had convinced me that I was an unloved stepchild of my heavenly Father. But now I see that I misunderstood Him completely."

Hundreds of women I've met live under the shadow of an "unpleasable" heavenly Father.

How would you describe your relationship with your Father? Is something still keeping you from reaching for what God wants to give you?

As we close this little book, ask the Holy Spirit to show you what unfinished business there might be between you and the Father. Ask Him to reveal anything that might be holding you back from responding wholeheartedly to His hand in your life.

You may be just one step away from the breakthrough you've wanted for years.

THE PLEASURE OF YOUR COMPANY

Sharon, another *Secrets* reader, wrote to say that she was struck with the statement that many Christians don't really believe God likes them. "How sad, and how true!" she wrote. "I see God as Someone who must be constantly disappointed in me, who is 'unpleasable,' instead of someone who really enjoys my company."

Sharon isn't alone. Hundreds of women I've met live under the shadow of an "unpleasable" heavenly Father. Whatever they might sing or say in church, these women go home to a God they believe is untrustworthy and unlikable. Yes, they believe God *loves* them—loving the world is His job, after all. But *like*? A Father who wants to be close to them *every minute of the day*? Impossible to imagine!

You can see how this common "heartsickness" would leave a Christian woman extremely reluctant to let the

Vinedresser anywhere near the branch of her life.

Do you believe in a God who really would enjoy the pleasure of your company? It's time to find out.

Bruce often uses a simple diagnostic chart that I've found helpful. It presents a series of words that describe God's attitude or feeling toward you. You mark the point on the scale that seems most accurate for you. Don't respond according to what you may have been taught. Respond according to how you honestly think and feel most of the time!

I THINK OF GOD AS:

STINGY   GENEROUS

| 1 | 2 | 3 | 4 | 5 | 6 | 7 | 8 | 9 | 10 |

HARSH   MERCIFUL

| 1 | 2 | 3 | 4 | 5 | 6 | 7 | 8 | 9 | 10 |

UNINTERESTED   ATTENTIVE

| 1 | 2 | 3 | 4 | 5 | 6 | 7 | 8 | 9 | 10 |

SHORT-TEMPERED   PATIENT

| 1 | 2 | 3 | 4 | 5 | 6 | 7 | 8 | 9 | 10 |

On which side of the scale do your choices fall? If your answers are lined up far to the right, you have an accurate picture of God. If your answers line up on the left, you probably identify with Sharon—which means that trusting the hand of the Vinedresser in your life will continue to seem impossible.

Let's look at a major common barrier in each season of a woman's life in the vineyard.

FEAR OF THE FATHER

Your greatest barrier to responding to God's discipline for ongoing sin might be fear. You might say, "Even if what I'm doing is wrong, I'm afraid to face God. What if He hurts me?"

The idea of fatherly discipline may have become emotionally tangled with chaos, violence, abuse, and neglect.

This response often stems from a negative experience with your own father or other father figure. "My father's idea of discipline," says Louise, "was to tell me I was ugly, fat, and no one would every marry me." Marli says, "Mostly I remember my stepdad's drunken rages and getting slapped so hard I flew across the room."

Sometimes a woman's response isn't so much fear as

emptiness. After Tami's mother left her father and moved across the country, her life changed radically. "My dad pretty much let me run wild," she said. "I don't think he really cared." Many others grow up in homes where a father is largely absent. *Father* becomes just another word for rejection and loss.

If you've had similar experiences growing up, the idea of fatherly discipline may have become emotionally tangled with chaos, violence, abuse, and neglect.

But our heavenly Father is different! Even in Bible times, the comparisons between earthly and heavenly father needed a little clarification. The writer of Hebrews contrasted the imperfect discipline of our earthly fathers, who could only do "as they thought best" with the life-giving discipline of God, which is "for our good" (Hebrews 12:10, NIV).

To let go of your old, broken idea of "father" and reach for a new one, you will need to open your heart to a healing truth: God is the perfect Father. Every time He intervenes in your life, His intention is to free you from a destructive choice that will take you in the wrong direction and away from Him. His actions are loving, tender, and wise—and the results are life giving.

That's why the Bible tells us never to despise or reject God's hand of discipline. Instead, we should "readily be in subjection to the Father of spirits *and live*" (Hebrews 12:9, emphasis added).

Consider these important truths about God's discipline:

- *Your heavenly Father's methods are perfect.* He never abuses His children. He's never too harsh or too lenient. He doesn't lose His temper. Exodus 34:6–7; Deuteronomy 1:30–31; Psalm 34.

- *Your heavenly Father's motives are perfect.* He is not trying to punish you or "even the score." He receives no personal satisfaction when He disciplines His "kids." Jeremiah 29:11; Ephesians 2:4–7; James 1:17.

- *Your heavenly Father's commitment is perfect.* He will actively pursue you, yet He honors your freedom of choice. What He wants most for you is what will bring you lasting fulfillment. Psalm 138; 1 Corinthians 1:26–29; 2 Peter 1:4.

- *Your heavenly Father's love for you is unconditional.* Your Father doesn't love you less because you're struggling with ongoing sin. He doesn't *like* you any less, either. His love for you is unending. Psalm 86:5; 2 Corinthians 1:3; 1 John 3:1.

If this is an area where you struggle, I encourage you to spend time with the Scriptures listed here. When you are ready, take the steps your Father is waiting for: Tell Him you will trust Him with your life, repent sincerely of the sin and misunderstandings that have kept you apart, and turn wholeheartedly in submission to Him. You can expect God to begin a beautiful healing process in your heart.

He has only a wonderful, fruitful future in mind for you, His precious child.

RESISTANCE TO HIS PLAN

A woman told me recently, "I would prefer to always be changed through pleasant and enjoyable circumstances." I understood her immediately, and I'm sure you do, too!

The most common barrier in pruning for women might be expressed like this: "Pruning feels too much like losing something important to me, *and I can't seem to let go.*"

Let that activity or attachment or possession go—He has something much better in mind for you.

If you're fearful or resistant about something God is trying to change in your life today, you will benefit from taking many of the same steps of trust I outlined for discipline in the previous section.

Even though you're not involved in an ongoing sin issue, your relationship with God is still hindered by your lack of trust in Him. And it takes trust—plus plenty of courage—to let go.

Yet the Bible says, "The works of His hands are faithful and just; all His precepts are trustworthy" (Psalm 111:7, NIV). "You are good, and what you do is good; teach me your decrees" (Psalm 119:68, NIV).

The breakthrough that's waiting for you is to choose to believe and act on a fundamental truth: *Your Father is good.* He is all-wise, all-loving, and all-powerful, and He is at work in you to redirect your energies toward a much more fruit-filled future than you can see at the moment.

We need to let go of a reliance on an emotional experience to prove to us that God is real or that He loves us.

With you specifically in mind, He has considered all the options, determined the most important area to focus on, and chosen the perfect time and method. That's what it means to be a perfect Father. And that's why you can trust Him enough to surrender to His pruning. So let that activity or attachment or possession go—He has something much better in mind for you. Accept the difficult time or season of suffering—God is in control, and He's at work in you for your *good.*

The same woman who confessed to wishing that God would bring only pleasant circumstances into our lives went on to say: "Of course, the lessons I've learned through the difficult times can't be compared with those I learned when everything was easy—if I learned anything at all. God has used tests of faith to get my preoccupation off of myself, and then He is able to show me more of Himself."

FREEDOM ABOUT FEELINGS

If abiding is the secret to the most spiritual abundance possible, and the only way to experience the deepest levels of intimacy with God, why do so few of us seem to succeed at it?

Based on what I've heard from Christian women over the years, I've concluded that one of the most common barriers to abiding could be described like this: *If I don't feel anything, nothing must be happening.*

Feelings do matter. God created you with emotions, and He cares about your heart. But if you assume abiding always brings with it a warm rush of feelings, then when you feel little or nothing, you'll decide you're not abiding. Soon you'll lose interest. Eventually, rather than deal with feelings of guilt and failure, you may give up altogether.

We all know, though, that emotional responses are determined by many factors—our physical condition, how much sleep we've had, whether we're anxious or depressed, how well we're getting along with our husband, whether we've had our morning coffee, the weather, our basic temperament type . . . it's a long list! And we don't judge our marriages or other significant friendships by feelings alone on any given day.

No wonder gauging intimacy with God by our emotions only eventually gets us in trouble.

Thankfully, emotion is a wonderful part of a genuine spiritual experience. Those feelings of exhilaration and release are God's gifts to us, and they inspire us to love Him more. Yet to grow toward maturity, we need to let go of a reliance on an emotional experience to prove to us that God is real or that He loves us.

The abiding breakthrough I invite you to make is to vow to pursue God in a sincere, respectful friendship for the rest of your life *no matter what you feel*. No other relationship could be as important, and none will ultimately be as fulfilling.

Every day, Jesus gives you an invitation: "Behold, I stand at the door and knock. If anyone hears My voice and opens the door, I will come in to him and dine with him, and he with Me" (Revelation 3:20).

Do you want Him to come in for a visit? Then keep opening that door every day of your life.

CHOSEN FOR GLORY

Did you know that grape plantings in California's Napa Valley often don't reach peak productivity for fifty years? Fruitfulness takes time. And overflowing abundance for God usually takes a lifetime.

But now you know that God *is* at work in you today! And you can be absolutely confident of this—"that He who has begun a good work in you will complete it until the day of Jesus Christ" (Philippians 1:6).

So no matter what season of life you're in today, be encouraged. Your future in God is a thing of beauty. And He is taking great delight in watching you grow.

Of course, on that day—not far from now—when you stand before Jesus with the fruit of your life, you probably won't see a single grape! Instead, you'll see faces. Your "fruit" will crowd around you with joy and celebration. In those faces you'll see your spouse, children, coworkers, family members, and neighbors you took one step closer to Christ. You'll see people around the world you haven't even met yet who were impacted by the commitments you made today.

> *When you stand before Jesus with the fruit of your life, you probably won't see a single grape! Instead, you'll see faces.*

You could see people God will bring into your path one hour from now!

On that day, when the Father looks at you and says, "Well done, good and faithful servant!" you'll know that your passion to bear fruit for His glory was the best decision you ever made as a child of God.

Take these vineyard teachings of Jesus with you in the very center of your heart as you continue your spiritual journey. Remember, you are loved unconditionally. You are being led each day into greater fulfillment and purpose for Him. And you have been chosen for abundance.

May your basket overflow!

Appendix

THREE SEASONS IN GOD'S VINEYARD

Distinctive Issues	THE SEASON OF **DISCIPLINE**	THE SEASON OF **PRUNING**	THE SEASON OF **ABIDING**
YOUR MAIN ARENA OF GROWTH	Sin	Self	Savior
GOD'S MAIN OBJECTIVE FOR YOU	Purify your behavior	Prioritize your values	Pursue your relationship with Him
WHAT GOD WANTS MOST FROM YOU	Obedience—to stop your sinning	Trust—to drop your distractions	Love—to deepen your friendship
WHAT YOUR BEST RESPONSE WOULD BE	Repentance	Relinquishment	Relationship
WHAT YOU SHOULD SAY WHEN YOU PRAY	*"Help me, Lord! Forgive me and deliver me from sin."*	*"Use me, Lord! Change me so I can do more for you."*	*"Draw me closer to You, Lord! Nothing else really matters but You!"*
WHAT YOU WILL EXPERIENCE	Restoration	Release	Rest
WHEN THIS SEASON WILL END	It ends when you stop the sin	It ends when you change your priorities	It doesn't have to end (God wants it to go on forever!)
WHAT GOD WANTS MOST TO GIVE YOU	Fruit from an obedient life	More fruit from a pruned life	Much fruit from an abiding life

SECRETS *of the* VINE
for Women

STUDY GUIDE

"I am the true vine, and My Father is the vinedresser. Every branch in Me that does not bear fruit He takes away; and every branch that bears fruit He prunes, that it may bear more fruit. You are already clean because of the word which I have spoken to you. Abide in Me, and I in you. As the branch cannot bear fruit of itself, unless it abides in the vine, neither can you, unless you abide in Me. I am the vine, you are the branches. He who abides in Me, and I in him, bears much fruit; for without Me you can do nothing."

JOHN 15:1–5, NKJV

CHAPTER ONE

A Spiritual Harvest

1. What words come to your mind when you think of an "abundant" life? What percentage of the women you know do you believe live an abundant life? Why do you think this is the case?

2. Look at the contrast Jesus makes in John 10:10. What does this tell you about what Jesus wants for our lives? What does it tell you about the real source of true abundance?

3. Can you recall a painful or difficult time in your life when you felt confused about what God was up to? What were your thoughts and feelings toward your situation, yourself, and God?

4. Looking back on a period of pruning in your life, can you identify any ways in which the experience resulted in personal growth or other benefits?

5. To what degree do you believe God is actively intervening in your life through circumstances or people you come into contact with?

6. Picture a continuum, with 1 being fate ("all of life just happens") and 10 being God ("He is directly responsible for all that happens in my life"). Where on the line does your belief rest? Note: There is no "right" answer, but either extreme is inaccurate. If your answer is 1 or 10, this book is going to be a surprise!

7. Describe why a person's belief that God is actively involved in her life is so important.

CHAPTER TWO

THE TOUCH
of ABUNDANCE

1. How do you respond to the truth that although salvation is a free gift by faith, God wants your life to produce something for Him?

2. Keeping in mind that God planned good works specifically for you to do, what kinds of activities do you feel uniquely gifted (based on your natural talents, abilities, and circumstances) to accomplish?

3. Read Titus 3:14. Paul equates good works with meeting "urgent needs." How does this definition change how you think about fruitfulness? Who do you know that has an urgent need you could help to meet this week?

4. How comfortable are you with placing a lot of emphasis on what you do or don't accomplish for God? Why do you think this is?

5. Read Matthew 5:16. What does Jesus say is the purpose of doing good works? Give some examples of what this might look like in a woman's life. What is the difference between this and good works done to be seen by men?

6. If you had to rate your level of fruitfulness for God right now, where would you place yourself?

7. How motivated are you to bear more fruit for God? Explain your answer.

CHAPTER THREE

LIFTED *by* LOVE

1. What emotions might be felt by a woman who consistently bears "no fruit"? Why?

2. Identify a time in your life when ongoing serious sin put you directly in the path of God's discipline. Did you recognize what was happening at the time? How did this affect your response?

3. If a woman believed that God will increase the intensity of discipline, why would she persist in sin?

4. God's discipline for specific sin ends as soon as we repent, but what kind of painful consequences might continue? Why is it so important to differentiate between the pain of natural consequences and that of discipline?

5. Share a time when God used a spoken warning (rebuke) in your life or in the life of someone you know. How did the person respond, and what was the result?

6. Look at James 4:17. What are some sins of commission and omission most prevalent among women?

7. Read Proverbs 3:12. What does God feel about you even as He is correcting you? How does knowing this change the way you think about His discipline?

CHAPTER FOUR

MAKING ROOM *for* MORE

1. What sort of activities might God want to prune from a woman's life? Why would these activities be considered "leaves"?

2. Discuss what might happen if we mistake God's pruning for discipline.

3. How has understanding spiritual pruning changed how you think about past painful experiences?

4. Can you look back on a time when you felt compelled to change your priorities for the better? Did you recognize that it was God at work? Did it lead to more fruit?

5. Read Philippians 1:12–14. Paul made a direct connection between hardships he'd endured and fruitfulness that resulted. Can you describe how a past season of pruning directly resulted in more fruit in your life?

6. The harder we hold onto something God is trying to prune, the more pruning comes...why do you suppose we so often struggle to let go?

7. Reflect on a time when you experienced a circumstance that God used to prune you. How long did it last? Why do you think God's pruning has different intensities and different lengths of time?

CHAPTER FIVE

THE MIRACLE *of* MUCH FRUIT

1. Think of a very close friend outside your immediate family. What qualities make that relationship meaningful and valuable to you? How much do you see these same qualities in your relationship with God?

2. Is the way you abide today different than a year ago? five years ago? Explain the difference.

3. Have you ever gone through a season in your Christian life when you made little or no effort to abide with Jesus? How did that feel, and what happened?

4. Can you identify with the mistake of wanting people you love to meet needs in your heart that only God can meet? Explain.

5. Read Matthew 11:28–30. How does what Jesus says here relate to the promise of abiding?

6. What are some unique challenges women today face when it comes to abiding?

7. What do you wish would be true about "abiding" for you? What steps can you take today to make this come to pass?

CHAPTER SIX

YOUR FATHER'S PRIZE

1. Why might it be important to avoid trying to determine whether another believer is being disciplined or pruned?

2. Is it difficult for you to believe that God not only loves you, He also *likes* you? Explain the difference and why you think many women find this a difficult concept.

3. How would you compare the parental discipline you received growing up to what you're learning about God's discipline? How do you think your past experiences still affect your response to God today?

4. When it comes to pruning, what are some practical things you could do to help yourself surrender something to God once and for all?

5. Read Mark 14:36 and Romans 8:15. God invites us to call Him "Abba Father." Why do you believe God teaches us that this kind of intimacy is possible?

6. Describe the role of faith in the choice to be more fruitful for God. Why is it so important?

7. Describe the way you want your life to look in one year in terms of fruitfulness and intimacy with God. Make a commitment to pray for one another accordingly.

PRAYER WITH A FEMININE EDGE
Ask for Extravagant Blessing

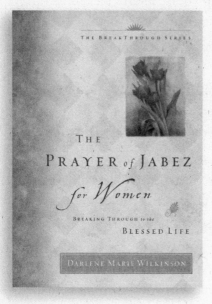

The phenomenal impact of *The Prayer of Jabez* is shown by reports of changed lives, expanded ministries, and spiritual breakthroughs among believers everywhere. Now women have their own unique version, written by Bruce Wilkinson's lifetime partner in marriage, that is full of significance for women's roles and ministry opportunities in God's kingdom. A must-read for every woman, whether she has read *The Prayer of Jabez* or not, this book addresses important questions, such as, *How can a busy mom expand her territory without neglecting the most important territory she already has, her family?* Darlene Marie Wilkinson's warm, personable approach reaches out to her reader, encouraging her to become like Jabez and experience the extraordinary life.

ISBN 1-57673-962-7

- The Prayer of Jabez for Women Audiocassette
- The Prayer of Jabez
- The Prayer of Jabez Audiocassette
- The Prayer of Jabez Audio CD
- The Prayer of Jabez Leather Edition
- The Prayer of Jabez Journal
- The Prayer of Jabez Devotional
- The Prayer of Jabez Bible Study
- The Prayer of Jabez Bible Study: Leader's Edition
- The Prayer of Jabez Gift Edition
- The Prayer of Jabez for Teens
- The Prayer of Jabez for Teens Audio CD